THE
TOWN CLOCK
BURNING

March 29, 1994

POEMS

Lucille,

Thank you

Keep Writing

By
CHARLES FORT

Carnegie Mellon University Press
Pittsburgh 1991

ACKNOWLEDGEMENTS

Some of these poems have appeared in the *Georgia Review,
Connecticut Writers Anthology, Argo, Road Apple Review, Huron
Review, Pontchartrain Review, Park River Review, Dark Waters,
Eclipse, Penny Dreadful, Bits and Pieces, White Jade, Writer-in-
Residence, Obsidan, Flute Song, Broadsides, Piscina Books, Panache,
Expressive Arts Review, Aftermath, Xavier Review, Portfolio 1983,
Crucible, St. Andrews Review, Anthology of American Verse,
International Poetry Review,* and *Cardinal Anthology.*

Publication of this book is supported by grants from the National
Endowment for the Arts in Washington D.C., a Federal agency, and
from the Pennsylvania Council on the Arts.

Library of Congress Catalog Card Number 91-70994
ISBN 0-88748-123-X
Printed and bound in the United States of America
Second Edition

FOR CHARLES........... *Father*
    CLARA............. *Mother*
    WENDY............ *Wife*
    CLAIRE............. *Daughter*

TABLE OF CONTENTS

O. HENRY AT HIS DESK / 1

WINTER KILL / 2

THUNDER FOR THE LADY'S SAKE / 3

THE WOMAN WHO DANCED WITHOUT MUSIC OR MEN / 4

NOVEMBER'S END / 5

HOMING PIGEON / 6

ANGEL NOBEL / 7

A PRAYER FOR WOMEN / 8

UNDERSTUDY / 9

THE WARNING (A Love Fable) / 10-11

POEM FOR BENJAMIN / 12

COLORATURA / 13

THE CARAVAN #1 / 14

THE CARAVAN #2 / 15

THE CARAVAN #3 / 16

THE CARAVAN #4 / 17

THE CARAVAN #5 / 18

PROSE POEM FOR CLAIRE AUBIN FORT / 19

FOR ROBERT HAYDEN / 20

SOMETHING CALLED A CITY (New Orleans) / 21

THE TOWN CLOCK BURNING / 22

FOR OUR TIME / 23

THE SHARE-CROPPERS / 24

RACE WAR / 25

REVIVAL, CUSTOM, CONTINENTS, ICON / 26

READING IT OVER AND OVER / 27

LIES IN THE GARDEN BEHIND THE LIBRARY / 28

TABLE OF CONTENTS (Continued)

MEMORIAL DAY FOR THE MILKMAN / 29

THE POET BURNING / 30

THE LOVER FROM ILLINOIS / 31

THE WEDDING MARCH (May 22, 1982) / 32

SILK KNIVES / 33

HOW OLD ARE THE PEOPLE OF THE WORLD / 34

FOR MAILER AND JACK / 35

THE USE OF FURNITURE
IN THE MOVEMENT OF BEN COCOA /36

BLUES OF A MUMBLING TRAIN / 37-38

FOR MARTIN LUTHER KING / 39

THE VELVET WOLF / 40

ARTICLES OF THE SEA DOG / 41

THE WORKER (We Own Two Houses) / 42

ONE HOUR / 43

CLARA / 44

LIFTING HIS ARMS / 45

ANCHOR-CITY (Mystic-Seaport, Connecticut) / 46

UMBRELLAS AND UNKNOWN LETTERS / 47-53

O. HENRY AT HIS DESK

We want to read how a just and miniature world
fell into the hands. The store-front church
and factory fall before the cypress and the pine.
Was his medal of honor a pawned star
pinned to his chest to keep the muse alive?

Certain births and deaths of citizens are left
unrecorded by the camera, census, and poem.
We acknowledge the writer and the gift a story
leaves to history and to those who part the roads
and build the sanctuary in a just and miniature world.

One believes in a story that extends
the hours of the living in a just and miniature world.
A writer can grant a wish to a traveler in a storm,
find tragedy in the perfect family photo,
flash forward and back, stall dreams.

In a just and miniature world
we want to pardon the writer,
reconstruct his story book endings,
interview the characters and rewrite
his chapters to match our own.

We can imagine how the pen
must have quaked in his fingers
and how the final words he wrote
ended his own life without surprise
in a just and minature world.

WINTER KILL

In winter there is one road
where nothing stops moving and the silver rings
inside ashen trees rotate with each sunset.
This is the road you will find me on.
I will kiss the wind slowly
until at the end of this road it sings.
This is the voice you will hear from me.
You will know by the steady reach of my arms
I am the vaulted shadow in wait.
This is the town you will find me in.
Under the shelter of your eyes,
in winter, I will fall into your arms like ash.

THUNDER FOR THE LADY'S SAKE

I search for you on a crusade journey
to Peru and Kenya with Inca-tools,
on islands, to large cities and poor towns
where the sunlight broods on the supple backs of workers
and constellations form large estates across the sky.
On small coasts the fish boats
bury themselves in edge-white sail,
coral sky, barren ground,
and one long shadow of a man.
I look at the air between two mountains,
their citadels tossed in heat
and your face becomes a distant blue miracle.
I am the beast resting upon your forehead.
I hold the pink eyes of your late grandmother.
I am the charmer tying knots of breath around your body.
The pearly nautilus web of light
has removed all of my blood,
and fear has changed the color of my eyes.
From these mountains I stand watching blackbirds
rise slowly and wait their return.

I gave them your name.
I gave them your name.

THE WOMAN WHO DANCED WITHOUT MUSIC OR MEN

I expected you
to disappear.
Suddenly dancing
without the necessary
equipment:
into the good weather
audience
and fresh applause
you danced.
I expected you
to disappear.
I stared
unable to define
weightless
and rolling to no
particular end.
A step behind
you danced.

NOVEMBER'S END

Two and a half minutes of snowfall
and you return wearing a pearl necklace,
gold and silver beads, a sapphire ring,
and a diamond watch on your wrist.

Will they take you to Cleveland or Boston
Connecticut or San Francisco?

Your child reaches over the steps
wanting more of you, his eyes widen
and when you touch him he laughs.

Will he know my face?
Who is that knocking at the door?
Are they coming for you?

Our dream house is tied to the ocean.
Bring it in closer.
We can carry it on our backs.

Each month I take as it ends
knowing somewhere in everyone's blood
pink leaves float and shadows are warm.

HOMING PIGEON

She flies with gold chips tied to her legs
the flight before her begging
traces of light and land and home.
Her pulse tacks wind.
On hollow bones
she estimates the loss of time
how she turns and where she flies.
She measures a distance
one can cover without air.

ANGEL NOBLE

You met him the day you were born
and there was a certain comfort in this;
the future suddenly cleared away
shreds of evidence your heart
could barely live on.
Were you his stray angel
who stared down on the world
willing to converse with the floating
heads of friends; the only one able
to retrieve thin wire embedded inside
the swollen minds of lovers?
You met him the day you were born.
The calculations of thunder in his eyes
embraced your heavenly human body
and there was a certain comfort in this.

A PRAYER FOR WOMEN

Perhaps born to red clay and thatch made her more than man.
A string of pearls in her mouth would not come alive
                            nor lengthen her dreams.
Perhaps for blood the pale tree of knowledge gave itself to her.
The shadows of breasts in the cave were for the grace of man.
Her children came out of her belly
like star-fish arms clinging to a round stone.
She carried her daughter and she walked her son to the shore.
Perhaps she gathered them like falling money in a cracked jar.

Perhaps she let them go, drowned them,
and stood naked before the moon and stars in reunion
                                with the sea.
Perhaps they were the black faces found buried
in the ghost towns of South Africa:
the white hands holding baskets of bread and wine
found smoldering in the bogs of Europe,
the yellow curled feet found on the mud farms of Asia,
the brown legs spread apart by phallic wonders
rising with each flag of this world.

UNDERSTUDY

In the final act
a voice over the phone
takes one year to reach me.
Is it her voice I hear?
I play another man's dream.
I hold a guitar whose sounds
are dark and borrowed.

THE WARNING (*A Love Fable*)

It was never easy for you
to forget the long love letter
the snapping clock above your brass bed
or the woman who pushed
a black and yellow baby carriage for hours
in and out of the room.

You have in your hands a shovel to search
for the heart of the woman you loved,
a heart buried separately, encased in gold,
by a soldier fifty-eight years ago.

At midnight you meet the seven
Ministers of the Heart,
tall and thin hollow men;
who warn if you should go on
follow the voices above your head,
who warn of the two
hind hooves of a wild horse,
who warn if you should fail
face death when it calls.

It was never easy for you to mention
the forty-five acres of land you acquired
somewhere in the rattle of Alabama.

You walk out of the Tavern of Fools
like a mantis arched for new territory,
lifting to sharpen, itching to destroy,
pulling apart the victim and rubbing
maple leaves for good times.

You come upon a piece of land nobody wanted
given up for no good with stories
hovering above its bottomless pits
made for the insane citizens to crawl
when nobody wanted them close by.

You separate this land from all other land
gather its stone and trees high in the mountains
turn up your eyes and throw down whatever is left.

You find a box near a brook
and before opening it you gather
teak-wood, garlic, mud and minnow.

Your walking this road at dawn
sifts the light of its breath and dust.

You open the box and her heart
rotates like a bladed disc.
You walk on. It is out of your hands.

POEM FOR BENJAMIN

Benjamin took his tools to Europe,
silver surfboard, pen and pencil,
sheets of song, half-alive on his
home-made destiny across the ocean.
From Connecticut to Breadloaf,
half-dead, in front of fireplaces
and writers like John Gardner,
his thundering white hair,
his long black pipe.
Your work-detail, Benjamin, minus
sweeping the rain, speaking in French,
and herding music notes on the mountains
was pulling hot steam out of clothes
picking loose buttons apart and making
the fringe stick to the sleeves.
We walked the Connecticut coastline
stepping across covered bridges,
stone cabbages, in piles, near roads
singed with completeness.
You wore crystal white beads
above dark flesh and black beard
to Europe across the ocean. . .

COLORATURA

The touch of a woman's lip
is a holiday for the burning leaves.
One feather falls through the pier's light;
a woman holding sand
walks until she realizes
the palms of leaves are falling
and there will be more waiting here.

THE CARAVAN # 1

It is a three year journey at night
pulling covered carts
full of diamonds, emeralds,
fowl and tired children
for ten thousand miles.
The large boxes on their backs
are filled with rock.
Nobody speaks out
and nothing can stop it.

Riding in the front
is the full-veiled woman
who danced without music or men.
Some talk low of how her hands
one night caught fire.
This princess crawled on her knees
and began digging those knotted bones
into the cool sand.

Others tell how her hands smoldered
and the wind carried the stench
through mountains.
The next day boar pigs arrived
rooting wild for some ungodly carcass
and inaccessible woman.
It is morning as the sun
becomes lit in white hair
and remains caught in this mirage of wind
until her deep set eyes are mine.

THE CARAVAN # 2

She captures uncommon birds
circling high wire thieves
against the calm press of night.
She takes each one separately.
She tears their wings and pushes
sticks through their eyes.

No one can rekindle
the language of her children
who know nothing but the ways
and sounds of killing.
They carry their princess a step
beyond the lunge-rock,
proceed until her skin
blisters under heat,
her totem heart secure.
The bones of her hands
and feet are thrown
into corners of her room.

They try to lower her body
into lake water
and knowing she will not go under
fall to their knees and pray:

The haunting fingers of this woman

the climbing　　　　　　*the climbing*

The mocking cry of this woman

the shaking　　　　　　*the shaking*

The silk scarves of this woman

the hiding　　　　　　*the hiding*

The thatched spirit of this woman

the living　　　　　　*the living*

The totem heart of this woman

the crowning　　　　　　*the crowning*

THE CARAVAN # 3

The caravan moves along the shore past moraine;
its children walk in chains at the ankles
as the sun begins to curse
and spin where scalpels
carved runic figures into their backs.

Winter is harsh and unexpected.
Thrown against the cold
some are left behind; these children
fall to the snow and rock
and crops soon grow through them.

Scaffolds are built.
many are tied to wood
and dropped into flames.
Unable to keep pace
some are dragged until the sea
washes out their eyes.

You are the children of our spirit
The first and last to leave this world

THE CARAVAN # 4

She sits in a corner
in a house made of string
and stares down at the scrolls
scattered under her feet.

She prays to her children:
Caves for the women
Eyes for the beast
Swords for the soldier
A child for the king

Inside the long corridors
her children tamper with jewels
dance and begin their dreams
washing their mouths with flowers.

THE CARAVAN # 5

Will a devil's dance
in their river huts
aboard cross sail vessels
with seams caulked in animal hair
carefully dipped in tar be enough?

The caravan moves out of history
its name carved into flame
at the center of zepher winds
where the sky enlarges all things.

The birds are screaming for their lives
The birds are screaming for their lives

PROSE POEM FOR CLAIRE AUBIN FORT
January 7, 3:23 a.m., 1985

Winter brings my wife a child, and your birth arrives
with the morning tide like wings alive in a jar. The
sunflower seeds and thorns bloom in your hands, Claire,
and we walk in the mist and draw circles in the sand.
I read your palms like a map, and there are small islands
and mountain roads rising in your summer eyes. Is my daughter
the dancer, actress, artist, gifted in language or song? I
search the form and proper length to write one impossible verse
to place into your hand. The unspoken metaphor falls like a
meteor into this simple throne of time I've built for you, and
your birth arrives with the morning tide like wings alive in a jar.

FOR ROBERT HAYDEN

Was it you walking in Vermont
underneath the arc of human color
escaping your own ashes;
or was it your shadow I watched
as the branches and flowers
fell apart at your touch;
or was it your waking hand
taut as a movement of light
held up against a mirror?

SOMETHING CALLED A CITY (New Orleans)

There are signals among a wreckage of flowers
struck clean in the earth's foaming hand.
something called a city
ruled by marching men, who sang and danced
and built their graves above the ground.
There are signals among a wreckage of humans
forced together naked and unafraid,
lost surveyors of night's crescent fall
bound by rope and fire.   The streets are rivers.
Who will unearth their gems and fat skulls?
There are signals without measure
like death uttered ten thousand years,
something called a city
ruled by marching men, who sang and danced
and built their graves above the ground.
There are brief signals
beginning and ending in the form of a child
with spiked fists and golden arms
who lifts a bird by its bright wing;
the ample, numbling, proof of power,
something called a city
ruled by marching men who sang and danced
and built their graves above the ground.

THE TOWN CLOCK BURNING

This clock positions each of us
in one square block behind the church.
Nothing has counted more and year after year
we march as it tells us to march.

This half-sleeping clock falters.
Its pendulum craves motion and time.
As powder and flame shadow each face
we guard what it tells us to guard.

Does this half-stepping wheel of fortune
know how a holy war begins?
What bell shaped terror   What moan?   What hour
we stop when it tells us to stop?

This is the clock of boundaries
marking its descent as its final seconds
pass into history and without pause
we harm what it tells us to harm.

FOR OUR TIME

December

We are caught
in sudden cold rain.

January

The open flesh of winter.
You whispered I'm yours.
Your voice, never strong,
disappeared with morning.
Razors cut outlines of heaven
into a young man's arm.

February

Our human hands
are forced together
as night and day.
Make way shadows
give them her eyes.

March

The fatal distance.
For our time
we ask too much.
My dark skin
made you wonder
who I was.
Your friends wondered
who you were.

April

Standing outside the gate
I wait and expect you back.
Lifting chips of thin slate
from the grass, I smile and begin
to snap off their calm edges.

THE SHARE-CROPPERS

They place seed and branches
on the edges of deep cut holes.
They plant once again
to gather the minute and hour
a low evening fire provides.

They come prepared with long knives to tear the ground.

RACE WAR (*For A. R.*)

We are carnal sinners blown about forever
like Hell proper's *Paolo* and *Francesca*.
We are face to face. We are reaching out
but we are not alive anymore, nothing like love
here tonight between races that moan, rocks that rise,
and a kindness that wounds and aches and whimpers.
This is a moment in history that refuses
to sit still, and our hands become great serpents
in a battle without victory. In this southern town
we exchange blows on our shapeless faces
until our eyes meet like playmates in a meadow.
We are children of circumstance, slave ships and reckless stars.
and there are few hours left in this world that *we may rise*
on stepping stones taking our dead selves to higher things.
We lead each other away from each other
odd and sightless creatures.
This moment is against us. Ripe and cunning,
earth is not sufficient and earth is our only companion.

*lines 15 (we may rise) and 16 (on stepping) from Tennyson's
In Memoriam

REVIVAL, CUSTOM, CONTINENTS, ICON

1.

We know the words well,
arena, high-water, and fear.
We keep to the ground
and sleep under the white moon
with slow voices in the cold morning.

2.

Love understood like stone
to a maker of buildings,
you are the equal operator
driller in the mid-rush to fame
un-holy collector of good will.

3.

I is eating chitlins and greens,
a handful of influential martyrs
and manchild brains for laughter,
to bring the world together.

4.

I am the Sage-Letter,
brimstone, feather in the wind
and the passion to contain it.
Carrier of new lines
erase this mis-thought.

READING IT OVER AND OVER

I turn each page and see through
each stage of her life; the scenery
always changes; black ink swells
inside her body; one page shows
Cleveland rising. On another page
Connecticut's landscape collapses
until the last page is only a word
and her thin shoulders begin folding
into wings as she looks down to ask
what else can happen
here.

LIES IN THE GARDEN BEHIND THE LIBRARY

You watch as they cut out the trees
and take away all that had grown for years
into small sacks against the fence.
You walk this same road at night
and the gnats are numerous.
Fear is everywhere in the heat.
Every star in one motion
Seems to shift across the sky behind you
following your patch into darkness.
There are thousands of on-going shadows
disintegrating and the resonance never stops.
It is night and the time for lies.

MEMORIAL DAY FOR THE MILKMAN

I choose not to press the bell
on the front door and knocked three or four times
before entering. The plants have names: Gwenivere, Skip,
Martini, Shevin. Some have died and others
stare out between thin shadows of warmth and cold
lifting their wings. Morning plays
the Third Act upon blank walls. The unsewn
pants and shirts are pushed into a bag.
Friends refuse to enter the two rooms
we leave behind. It will get to you soon enough.
It will be a simple act.

THE POET BURNING

Only the poet stood to tell
what happened here, happened to the world,
fear of angels, empty tombs, falling stars.
I turn pages from a book written
before the first spoken word, *becos,*
before the flames engulfed the city and forest.
I caress the cold element
where the shadows of the dead
meet the passions of the living.
I watch how both are thrown together
like a cruel hour of history
crawling out of the seed and web of ice
thrown by the laughter of the mountains.
I turn pages where, in living, these dangers
remain calm fiction in front of a mirror.
Blown three circles from the birthplace of dawn
only the poet stood to tell
what happened here, happened to the world.
The poet, on all fours, sheds his living fur,
fear of angels, empty tombs, falling stars.

THE LOVER FROM ILLINOIS

I walk behind you.
I dance and whisper down
the square-dark staircase.
I stand behind the windswept moon
and the soldier on the mountain
under a shower of pearls
washed and sculptured like blown glass.
There is a gray shallow pool
reflecting my face and the trees
and there is bitter light in your hands.

THE WEDDING MARCH *May 22, 1982*

Our mothers pray before the altar of blossoms
holding wedding candles burning mahogany light
in the happenstance of arms attending arms,
forever proud, centered, and single file.
Their only wish to give their wish away
to the feathered ape who flips backward
down a long aisle in their doll's house
and places the ringed apparition
on his lover's hand.

SILK KNIVES

From the window
the shifting ice unfolds.
The sun relaxes on its surface
and light moves off center,
the glitter, the moment, removed.
Silk knives are shaken loose
from rising mist.
Black trees gather form
and our lives unexpectingly fuse.

HOW OLD ARE THE PEOPLE OF THE WORLD

They are scattered ageless souls
urging the minutes and hours to cease,
mere shadows in their aching slumber
rising like temples born out of fire.
They are blind survivors traveling primitive waters
rescued from the only god they knew
by a child willing to ask how old
are the people of the world, a child able
to see how twilight releases its carpentry:
yesterday the stars were gold coins spinning to earth.
They are shapes thrown together by the rattled eye
driven like a memory lost in its own fever,
telling as a town crier flying death's carriage
drawn into the belly pool of time.
It is winter becoming winter again.
Blue fog cuts the tops of trees,
dispersed, October, still moving
unrelating as eyes searching out food
as the man to first raise his hand for blood
kicking the locust for its very idea.

FOR MAILER AND JACK

He never intended to stab.
The act came on suddenly
and smoothly.
He never understood
why he murdered.
The victim had not been a friend
well dressed and respected.

Maybe in the past.
Maybe in the past.
A bad feeling inside.
Why he murdered
he never understood.

He turned away slowly
as if nothing mattered
and never understood.

THE USE OF FURNITURE
IN THE MOVEMENT OF BEN COCOA

Ben Cocoa, alias,
The Amazing Petrified Man,
rode the rails a one-legged black hobo
who died trying to leap for a home.
The train didn't stop
and a carnival kept up the pace
his body in a state of shock
from town to town the show of shows.

Ben Cocoa thought only of these words:
I am afraid of being made into bacon.
I am scared of the hell that follows.
I am afraid of being placed in a bottle
I am scared of the hell that follows.

Ben Cocoa,
the down home invisible hobo
was thrown from a train.
He must have been dreaming:

I am two hundred
and fifty years old
with a small heart in my chest
and I'll be dying soon.

BLUES OF A MUMBLING TRAIN
(The Underground Railroad)

What brings the flash of a sword
near the innocent, pulls on their bodies
and holds them to the sun?
The Fugitive Slave Bill 1850

An Act Respecting Fugitives
From Justice and Persons
Escaping from Servitude
Of Their Masters

Arriving from: Richmond, Norfolk, New Orleans, Dorchester
County, South Carolina, Hartford County,
Washington, D.C., Chicago, Prince George's
County.

Joe T. White
Would rather fight than eat.

Perry Johnson
Eye knocked out.

Charles Gilbert

Fleeing From Davis, A Negro Trader, Secreted Under A Hotel,
Up a Tree, Under A Floor, In A Thicket On A Steamer.

They travel past old towns
peering through cracks
in mail rooms and rail cars;
newspapers mold in corners
near the furnace and obituaries
on page two are names without faces:

37

Harper Parker Rache
Pennypacker Gilbert Garrison
Gibbons Cleveland Rhoads
White McKim Johnson
Fussell Goodwin Garrett

Purvis Furness
Mott Marian
Shipley Moore
Hopper Burris
Corson Miller

Harriet Tubman

The porter-of-promise and his bulging hands
gathers coins to buy a long
silver necklace for his daughter's neck.
She is the shout song of history
crawling on grass painted blue
in silhouetted water; she brushes
against the hillside, past castles where men
in armor whistle as she only nods
and speaks as few words; her eyes
empty forth images; coachmen
riding rail cars whip against her frame mist.
she is the reckless ship at sea.

Mary Epps alias Emma Brown

Slave mother loses her speech
at the sale of her child.
She screams from the rooftop,
third year in Chicago
without her child.
Hold to the earth woman;
let your ghost-town go,
a denied home, broken wings,
ice-age time in southern streams.

FOR MARTIN LUTHER KING

Black swans with wings over their eyes
move out on a simple road
and flourish in their song.
They lead a memorial search-light
into America's backyard
against the stout sheriff and water hose
and they march face to face
toward foes with their empty hands.
They push their hands
into the soil, and brush over
the ears and lips of Martin's mask.
America, does it take a stage coach
ambulance, moist engine of fear,
to call out his name?

THE VELVET WOLF

A nightwatch over its spirit
would not save our village
only the velvet touch
above the wolf's neck

We stare unable to define its crown
or the thin line where our eyes meet.
We pace to the sharpening of teeth
as the loner renews its thirst
until only its howl need clear this mountain.

ARTICLES OF THE SEA-DOG

I brush the frost from my coat.
I hold my hands tight enough to drink.
I carry the weight of her eyes.
I turn colors like a whip.
I carry congo drums and teaspoons.
I merge with a thousand blue Indians.
I merge frightless and unashmed.
I tamper night with rain.
I ride horseback plain horseback.
I am headed where light travels slowly.
I see a blindspot on this earth.
I am the judge, the courts, the law.
I sit wearing a blue hood and a white robe.
I walk where armies once marched.
I hear morning's fallen leaves captured and howling
I shape the harvest and the sweet universe.
Could my hands build such a large stone?
I dream winter on a city block.
I live in palaces and low rent apartments.
I hold newspapers I have yet to read.
I take the earth and carve out the sky.
I walk neighborhood shops and wrestling shows.
I watch window swimming lobsters.
I pull the cart from the mud.
I need telepathy and half-moons to guide.
I run behind wet footprints.
I have the face of unknown soldiers.
I am the angel tipping drinks.
I am the devil laughing.
I am the names of ships that limp inside.
I am a child begging the world for good sleep.

THE WORKER (We Own Two Houses)

My father was a barber-surgeon
for thirty-three years
and a factory worker
for eighteen of those years.

On Saturdays it seemed as if
the entire Negro section of town
had grown long hair.
The sounds of shears
still vibrate my ears.
I swept clouds into the wastebasket.
The back room contained hard whiskey
bookies and hidden magazines.

When my father came home at seven a.m.
lifting his black aluminum lunch box,
we seven children met him at the door,
knelt, and untied his shoes.
His tired eyes reflected
into the side of that box.
Each of us wanted left-overs;
we grew older and took turns.
Steel ball-bearings turned in his hands,
given to us as marbles
and the largest on the block.

They made my father a supervisor;
his white friends for eighteen years
now turned from his voice.
Years before the Army
broke his legs in basic training,
fused them for life.

When dust began to fill my father's bones,
I learned how chronic arthritis
can lock together any old man.
From the backroom I heard my name
and a razor being slapped against leather.
With magazines thrown into place
I carried out his clean towels.
I picked up clouds.

ONE HOUR

I stand in a storm at eleven p.m.
and take time to laugh out
my own story: the nurses
hold down sheets on the cancer
inside mother's left breast above the heart.
It is eleven fifteen.
Tonight red clay burns in the loin of the mountain
like a soldier's idle triumph of the flesh.
It is eleven forty-five.
Do I believe the doctor's call?
I am punctual and masculine as nerves in a fist
beating drums and idols made of wood on the cancer
inside mother's left breast above the heart.
It is eleven-fifty-nine and to hell with chance.
I stride into her room
and shake off the moist drill of this season,
believing the timid surgeon's minstrel hands
guard the living well.

CLARA

a daughter's mother
a son's girl
grandma's lady in life

She gave seven children
what this world could never return;
between the dirty laundry
out of seven bold babies,
between our nightmares
and falling out of bed.
She gave what this world
could never return: Clara.

a daughter's mother
a son's girl
grandma's lady in life.

LIFTING HIS ARMS

Grandfather was there lifting his arms.
Dusklight from the window
burned his eyes. He was awake.
In his basement room
African artifacts choked evil,
sixteen carved faces in strawbags
hung low from the ceiling, the wool blanket,
a stick patch across his chest.
I watched death there
jut its long draped self out of a corner
and spiral into a whisper one might talk to.
Fever shook his venom fired hand
each rising vein caught between
a backyard breeze every blackened tree,
this field, his wish, a movement of the stars.

ANCHOR-CITY (Mystic Seaport, Connecticut)

1.

The rockmast
Fell at noon
She had to begin living
Red clouds
Settled into her skin
Griffin birds circled
Above her head
Shifting stars
Captured and howling
Set pace for new land.

2.

Attempts to salvage
The hush boat
At Mystic-Seaport
Graystones at rest
Her boneless breathing
Alien to nature
Half the secluded world
Danced at her side
Blisters wore heavy
Step lightly where you go.

3.

She drags to shore
A palace preserved
No sign of life
The raft drifts empty
Rising   gone
Would she start
This far out from land
Give her final word
To throw roses to water gods
Into their sweet laugh?

UMBRELLAS AND UNKNOWN LETTERS

Awakened, mother answers the phone.
It is November, 1960. "Don't vote for him,
Kennedy the traitor, nigger lover."
Behind a voice so clear
believing her white the caller came through.
It has taken twenty-four years to breath this out.

Today, ladies and gentlemen,
the President will jog off the edge of the earth
and every old person will be found
in the fields frozen to death
The World Bank of England will paste
the Magna Carter to its safe
and beg another thousand years
there will be silence over New Orleans
where the rain will fall like war
as people wait for nets to carry them out
Encouraging signs will read: Homes for Sale
I am institutionalized.
I am born to bleed.
The U.S.A is now open 9 to 5 Sundays
during this time there will be a slide show on **Viet-Nam**
for the defoliated demilitarized minds
at the Public Library with your own brother
now 41 and dead you will see in his face
on Video Replay that it did no good to fight
because simply somebody had to die
Did caring or knowing the misfunctions
in the judges the courts the laws
help Attica?   The U.S.A. is now
closed for repairs and you Miss Liberty
can kiss the doorways to Harlem
and shed all the tears I leave
them far behind The last Prisoner of all Wars
walks steadfast half amazed

half model clay with arms folded
a back pack and the long red cuts
down his back

From his long history:
the mythic negro as mythic hero

he was good looking used twelve cans
of deodorant a week. He was good looking
shining brown mare cornhusk hair
barn at the side of a rocking chair, indeed.
A member of the black race? He was good looking,
free from all ethnic background.
I can't keep the pace   Can't eat
My eyes full of mace   Can't dance
Can't even play dice in my dreams
where old men dwell like sea-horses

From his long history:
I can see myself rigid and righteous

in the fields of Africa falling against
the tightened skin of a manic beast
I can see myself thrown into rivers
I can live the lonely dreams
my dreams
unconquered dreams
dreams of dreams
my greed
my unconquered greed
dreams of greed
my dreams
made it no better
living the lonely dreams
washing down babies dressed in Zebra cloth
belonging to the Great X X X X
Where was I when tribes

brought home food for the hungry?

From his long history:

The Amistad
The reading of stars began on this slaveship
genocide express moving in figure eight
a child's statellite filling one by with men's lives

From his long history:
A glory Stomp

Slums are made
marketed and sold to maintain the coolness
found in street bars and juke boxes, meantime,
to live like a jewel out of Madison Avenue
become exempt from everyday marital relationships
build inferior housing with bookies on the run
sell life insurance to the pusher or the pimp
together can develop anybody
into the Father of their Country
Slums are made and marketed and sold
to last, but you can take a ride
from Watts to Disney Land

From his long history:
Inside New York City

subway trains hold mute aliens
electrified, star-borne, and bronzed

From his long history:
the barbecue

I ran for miles and saw one man
named, Rufus SideStreet, a community builder,
lose his mind his dinner his shoes
He was a precious stone made of steam

He was the champ, open toed, and fire
Snake of a thousand lands
Such a walk
Such a way to die
corner kid plays tiger games
falls on dodge ball
rescued by mountainous band-aid
The cellar door inhales dust
rotting stairs and aging tools
the faucet water browns
grey yellow topped grasshoppers
bounce off summer screens
a charcoal mist consumes automobiles
and dead pets covering the valley
I watch the food cooking

From his long history:
there came gettysburg

and miles of marches a flow of petty cash
horns and drums for children
Today, Wilmington, North Carolina,
will be visited by a fleet of water boats
sailing for the New World
where citizens on board
tell stories of puppies and stolen lunches
and converse with, Neptune, King of the Cape Fear River
Dreams of nuclear plants penetrate our lives,
a bent rusted tire hammer is all that is left of the world

From his long history:
Turning back to White Flight and Favour

sixteen black men or the Wilmington Ten
dos'-a-dos'   dos'-a-dos'
one step forward   one step back
take your partner white or black
sixteen black men laying eggs like hens
dos-a-dos'   dos'-a-dos'
back to back   face to face

take your partner white or black
sixteen black men laying eggs like hens
Today, ladies and gentlemen,
is also the kidnapping of master jones bones
and the naked reunion of Charlie Parker
with Patricia Hearst riding off from Watts to Camelot
one step forward   one step back
into quicksand and their untimely demise
is noticed by sixteen black men sitting in a pie
These men will be plainly speaking:

SLA	Sleep	Late	Always
FBI	Fabulous	Bacon	Inside
SLA	Sex	Laxative	Anarchy
FBI	Fabian	Baseball	Ice

On a cool July Evening I listen
to Mahalia Jackson once every millenium
GM builds robots that sing the blues
the last mountain true to itself flashed
its echo to this ancient city
From city hall smoke rings rise and circle Market Street
Twenty one minutes before rush hour
suburban blind mice
with their long red tongues caught
in the steering wheels of honda civics
cross into elite land and throw
from their car windows slices of Wonder Bread
for city pigeons and city chickens
dressed in long silk robes and strut
their asses high out of the city . . .
This storm-shed city will search you out
missing the Mardi Gras will not be a joke
there will be the World KKK again, and another
passive president who feels nothing every four years
says nothing every four years and holds the flag
at his whim and there will be yet another war
the cause unknown it is known however
that all the dead and injured will be wearing white

hats and green shoes for exact identification

From his long history:
inside South Africa's

Diamond mines, all African men
become three feet tall
with Diamond Dust running through their blood
their copper covered hands drill through stone
their eyes blister from the darkness
and shut tight when the sun rises
Their Big Boss
heats and freezes their souls
He wants no one to speak out talk back
or to visit their gods
These are the faces of summer in blackmask
holding on they accept nothing
praying they sit for years waiting
monumental desperate raging
Washington Moscow Washington Moscow
The animal heart and alchemy

How does your metal grow?
Washington Moscow Washington Moscow

The animal heart and alchemy
How does your metal grow?

From his long history:
the long senseless creation of war

drags on   drags on
War for this and War for that
Simple Simon rules the universe
of the mad and simple men
but night is fragile biting our minds for sleep
The statues of MAY DAY MAY DAY
glitter and struggle under the rubbish

The shining in our lives recedes
and breaks tempo with the earth
Stars shake
We climb into the burning bush to listen
New Faculty New Land New Life
It is time to sit still
The tax man pulls the drink from my hand
It is time to leave
this blue room out the blue door into the blue world
Today ladies and gentlemen your fine gold teeth
formerly guarding the Pentagon will be found floating in hell
and then I will take my rest world
cherish and believe in all that is lovely
but if you still cannot remember that half loaf of bread
laying on of hands is for quote all god's children unquote
for each and every child there will be there will only be
a quiet sunrise in winter left to kill.